CW00508335

2017 SQA Specimen and Past Papers with Answers

National 5
MATHEMATICS

2016 & 2017 Exams
and 2017 Specimen Question Paper

HODDER
GIBSON
AN HACHETTE UK COMPANY

This book contains the official SQA 2016 and 2017 Exams, and the 2017 Specimen Question Paper for National 5 Mathematics, with associated SQA-approved answers modified from the official marking instructions that accompany the paper.

In addition the book contains study skills advice. This advice has been specially commissioned by Hodder Gibson, and has been written by experienced senior teachers and examiners in line with the new National 5 syllabus and assessment outlines. This is not SQA material but has been devised to provide further guidance for National 5 examinations.

Hodder Gibson is grateful to the copyright holders, as credited on the final page of the Answer section, for permission to use their material. Every effort has been made to trace the copyright holders and to obtain their permission for the use of copyright material. Hodder Gibson will be happy to receive information allowing us to rectify any error or omission in future editions.

Hachette UK's policy is to use papers that are natural, renewable and recyclable products and made from wood grown in sustainable forests. The logging and manufacturing processes are expected to conform to the environmental regulations of the country of origin.

Orders: please contact Bookpoint Ltd, 130 Park Drive, Milton Park, Abingdon, Oxon OX14 4SE. Telephone: (44) 01235 827720. Fax: (44) 01235 400454. Lines are open 9.00–5.00, Monday to Saturday, with a 24-hour message answering service. Visit our website at www.hoddereducation.co.uk. Hodder Gibson can be contacted direct on: Tel: 0141 333 4650; Fax: 0141 404 8188; email: hoddergibson@hodder.co.uk

This collection first published in 2017 by
Hodder Gibson, an imprint of Hodder Education,
An Hachette UK Company
211 St Vincent Street
Glasgow G2 5QY

National 5 2016 and 2017 Exam Papers and Answers; 2017 Specimen Question Paper and Answers © Scottish Qualifications Authority. Study Skills section © Hodder Gibson. All rights reserved. Apart from any use permitted under UK copyright law, no part of this publication may be reproduced or transmitted in any form or by any means, electronic or mechanical, including photocopying and recording, or held within any information storage and retrieval system, without permission in writing from the publisher or under licence from the Copyright Licensing Agency Limited. Further details of such licences (for reprographic reproduction) may be obtained from the Copyright Licensing Agency Limited, www.cla.co.uk

Typeset by Aptara, Inc.

Printed in the UK

A catalogue record for this title is available from the British Library

ISBN: 978-1-5104-2195-0

2 1

2018 2017

Introduction

National 5 Mathematics

This book of SQA past papers contains the question papers used in the 2016 and 2017 exams (with answers at the back of the book). The National 5 Mathematics exam is being extended by 20 marks for 2018 onwards, following the removal of unit assessments from the course. A new specimen question paper, which reflects the requirements of the revised exam, is also included. The specimen question paper reflects the content and duration of the exam in 2018.

All of the question papers included in the book (2016, 2017 and the new specimen question paper) provide excellent representative exam practice for the final exams. Using the 2016 and 2017 past papers as part of your revision will help you to develop the vital skills and techniques needed for the exam, and will help you to identify any knowledge gaps you may have.

It is always a very good idea to refer to SQA's website for the most up-to-date course specification documents. These are available for each subject at www.sqa.org.uk/nqsubjects

The course

The National 5 Mathematics course aims to enable you to develop the ability to:

- select and apply mathematical techniques in a variety of mathematical and real-life situations
- manipulate abstract terms in order to solve problems and to generalise
- interpret, communicate and manage information in mathematical form
- use mathematical language and explore mathematical ideas.

Before starting this course you should already have the knowledge, understanding and skills required to achieve a good pass in National 4 Mathematics and/or be proficient in equivalent experiences and outcomes. This course enables you to further develop your knowledge, understanding and skills in algebra, geometry, trigonometry, numeracy, statistics and reasoning. The course content is summarised below.

Algebra	Geometry		Trigonometry
<ul><li>Expanding brackets</li><li>Factorising</li><li>Completing the square</li><li>Algebraic fractions</li><li>Equation of straight line</li><li>Functional notation</li><li>Equations and inequations</li><li>Simultaneous equations</li><li>Change of subject of formulae</li><li>Graphs of quadratic functions</li><li>Quadratic equations and discriminant</li></ul>	<ul><li>Gradient</li><li>Volume</li><li>Properties of shapes</li><li>Vectors and 3D coordinates</li></ul>	<ul><li>Arc and sector of circle</li><li>Pythagoras' theorem</li><li>Similarity</li></ul>	<ul><li>Graphs</li><li>Equations</li><li>Identities</li><li>Area of triangle, sine rule, cosine rule, bearings</li></ul>
	Numeracy		**Statistics**
	<ul><li>Surds</li><li>Indices and scientific notation</li><li>Rounding (significant figures)</li><li>Percentages</li><li>Fractions</li></ul>		<ul><li>Semi-interquartile range, standard deviation</li><li>Scattergraphs; equation of line of best fit</li></ul>
Reasoning			
<ul><li>Interpreting a situation where mathematics can be used and identifying a strategy.</li><li>Explaining a solution and/or relating it to context.</li></ul>			

Assessment

The course assessment is an examination comprising two question papers.

The number of marks and the times allotted for the examination papers are as follows:

Paper 1 (non-calculator)	50 marks	1 hour 15 minutes
Paper 2	60 marks	1 hour 50 minutes

The course assessment is graded A-D, the grade being determined by the total mark you score in the examination.

Some tips for achieving a good mark

- **DOING** maths questions is the most effective use of your study time. You will benefit much more from spending 30 minutes doing maths questions than spending several hours copying out notes or reading a maths textbook.
- Practise doing the type of questions that are likely to appear in the exam. Work through these practice papers and similar questions from past Credit Level and Intermediate 2 papers. Use the marking instructions to check your answers and to understand what the examiners are looking for. Ask your teacher for help if you get stuck.
- **SHOW ALL WORKING CLEARLY.** The instructions on the front of the exam paper state that "Full credit will only be given where the solution contains appropriate working". A "correct" answer with no working may only be awarded partial marks or even no marks at all. An incomplete answer will be awarded marks for any appropriate working. Attempt every question, even if you are not sure whether you are correct or not. Your solution may contain working which will gain some marks. A blank response is certain to be awarded no marks. Never score out working unless you have something better to replace it with.

- Communication is very important in presenting solutions to questions. Diagrams are often a good way of conveying information and enabling markers to understand your working. Where a diagram is included in a question, it is often good practice to copy it and show the results of your working on the copy.
- In Paper 1, you have to carry out calculations without a calculator. Candidates' performance in number skills is often disappointing, and costs many of them valuable marks. Ensure that you practise your number skills regularly, especially within questions testing Course content.
- In Paper 2, you will be allowed to use a calculator. Always use **your own** calculator. Different calculators often function in slightly different ways, so make sure that you know how to operate yours. Having to use a calculator that you are unfamiliar with on the day of the exam will disadvantage you.
- Prepare thoroughly to tackle questions from **all** parts of the course. Numerical and algebraic fractions, graphs of quadratic fractions, surds, indices and trigonometric identities are topics that often cause candidates problems. Be prepared to put extra effort into mastering these topics.

Some common errors to avoid

	Common error	Correct answer
Converse of Pythagoras' Theorem e.g. Prove that triangle ABC is right angled. A, 3, 5, B, 4, C (triangle diagram)	Don't start by assuming what you are trying to prove is true. $AC^2 = AB^2 + BC^2$ $AC^2 = 3^2 + 4^2 = 9 + 16 = 25$ $AC = \sqrt{25} = 5$ so triangle ABC is right angled by the Converse of Pythagoras' Theorem.	Don't state that $AC^2 = AB^2 + BC^2$ until you have the evidence to prove that it is true. $AC^2 = 5^2 = 25$ $AB^2 + BC^2 = 3^2 + 4^2 = 9 + 16 = 25$ so $AC^2 = AB^2 + BC^2$ so triangle ABC is right angled by the Converse of Pythagoras' Theorem.
Similarity (area and volume) e.g. 5cm, 10cm (two cylinders) Theses cylinders are mathematically similar. The volume of the small one is $60cm^3$. Calculate the volume of the large one.	Don't use the linear scale factor to calculate the volume (or area) of a similar shape. Scale factor = 2 Volume = $2 \times 60 = 120cm^3$	Remember that volume factor = (linear factor)^3 area factor = (linear factor)^2 Scale factor = 2 Volume = $2^3 \times 60 = 480cm^3$
Reverse use of percentage e.g. After a 5% pay rise, Ann now earns £252 per week. Calculate her weekly pay before the rise.	Increase = 5% of old pay **NOT** 5% of new pay Increase = 5% of £252 = £12·60 Old pay = £252 - £12·60 = £239·40	New pay = (100% + 5%) of old pay New pay = 105% of old pay = £252 1% of old pay = £252 ÷ 105 = £2·40 Old pay = 100% = £2·40 × 100 = £240
Interpreting statistics e.g. Jack and Jill sat tests in the same eight subjects. Jack's mean mark was 76 and his standard deviation was 13. Jill's mean mark was 59 and her standard deviation was 21. Make two valid comments comparing the performance of Jack and Jill in the tests.	This answer does not show that you **understand** the meaning of mean and standard deviation. Jack has a higher mean mark but a lower standard deviation than Jill.	Your interpretation of the figures must show that you **understand** that mean is an average and that standard deviation is a measure of spread. On average Jack performed better than Jill as his mean mark was higher. Jack's performance was more consistent than Jill's as the standard deviation of his marks was lower.

Good luck!

Remember that the rewards for passing National 5 Mathematics are well worth it! Your pass will help you get the future you want for yourself. In the exam, be confident in your own ability, if you're not sure how to answer a question trust your instincts and just give it a go anyway – keep calm and don't panic! GOOD LUCK!

Study Skills – what you need to know to pass exams!

Pause for thought

Many students might skip quickly through a page like this. After all, we all know how to revise. Do you really though?

Think about this:

"IF YOU ALWAYS DO WHAT YOU ALWAYS DO, YOU WILL ALWAYS GET WHAT YOU HAVE ALWAYS GOT."

Do you like the grades you get? Do you want to do better? If you get full marks in your assessment, then that's great! Change nothing! This section is just to help you get that little bit better than you already are.

There are two main parts to the advice on offer here. The first part highlights fairly obvious things but which are also very important. The second part makes suggestions about revision that you might not have thought about but which WILL help you.

Part 1

DOH! It's so obvious but …

Start revising in good time

Don't leave it until the last minute – this will make you panic.

Make a revision timetable that sets out work time AND play time.

Sleep and eat!

Obvious really, and very helpful. Avoid arguments or stressful things too – even games that wind you up. You need to be fit, awake and focused!

Know your place!

Make sure you know exactly **WHEN and WHERE** your exams are.

Know your enemy!

Make sure you know what to expect in the exam.

How is the paper structured?

How much time is there for each question?

What types of question are involved?

Which topics seem to come up time and time again?

Which topics are your strongest and which are your weakest?

Are all topics compulsory or are there choices?

Learn by DOING!

There is no substitute for past papers and practice papers – they are simply essential! Tackling this collection of papers and answers is exactly the right thing to be doing as your exams approach.

Part 2

People learn in different ways. Some like low light, some bright. Some like early morning, some like evening / night. Some prefer warm, some prefer cold. But everyone uses their BRAIN and the brain works when it is active. Passive learning – sitting gazing at notes – is the most INEFFICIENT way to learn anything. Below you will find tips and ideas for making your revision more effective and maybe even more enjoyable. What follows gets your brain active, and active learning works!

Activity 1 – Stop and review

Step 1

When you have done no more than 5 minutes of revision reading STOP!

Step 2

Write a heading in your own words which sums up the topic you have been revising.

Step 3

Write a summary of what you have revised in no more than two sentences. Don't fool yourself by saying, "I know it, but I cannot put it into words". That just means you don't know it well enough. If you cannot write your summary, revise that section again, knowing that you must write a summary at the end of it. Many of you will have notebooks full of blue/black ink writing. Many of the pages will not be especially attractive or memorable so try to liven them up a bit with colour as you are reviewing and rewriting. **This is a great memory aid, and memory is the most important thing.**

Activity 2 – Use technology!

Why should everything be written down? Have you thought about "mental" maps, diagrams, cartoons and colour to help you learn? And rather than write down notes, why not record your revision material?

What about having a text message revision session with friends? Keep in touch with them to find out how and what they are revising and share ideas and questions.

Why not make a video diary where you tell the camera what you are doing, what you think you have learned and what you still have to do? No one has to see or hear it, but the process of having to organise your thoughts in a formal way to explain something is a very important learning practice.

Be sure to make use of electronic files. You could begin to summarise your class notes. Your typing might be slow, but it will get faster and the typed notes will be easier to read than the scribbles in your class notes. Try to add different fonts and colours to make your work stand out. You can easily Google relevant pictures, cartoons and diagrams which you can copy and paste to make your work more attractive and **MEMORABLE**.

Activity 3 – This is it. Do this and you will know lots!

Step 1

In this task you must be very honest with yourself! Find the SQA syllabus for your subject (www.sqa.org.uk). Look at how it is broken down into main topics called MANDATORY knowledge. That means stuff you MUST know.

Step 2

BEFORE you do ANY revision on this topic, write a list of everything that you already know about the subject. It might be quite a long list but you only need to write it once. It shows you all the information that is already in your long-term memory so you know what parts you do not need to revise!

Step 3

Pick a chapter or section from your book or revision notes. Choose a fairly large section or a whole chapter to get the most out of this activity.

With a buddy, use Skype, Facetime, Twitter or any other communication you have, to play the game "If this is the answer, what is the question?". For example, if you are revising Geography and the answer you provide is "meander", your buddy would have to make up a question like "What is the word that describes a feature of a river where it flows slowly and bends often from side to side?".

Make up 10 "answers" based on the content of the chapter or section you are using. Give this to your buddy to solve while you solve theirs.

Step 4

Construct a wordsearch of at least 10 × 10 squares. You can make it as big as you like but keep it realistic. Work together with a group of friends. Many apps allow you to make wordsearch puzzles online. The words and phrases can go in any direction and phrases can be split. Your puzzle must only contain facts linked to the topic you are revising. Your task is to find 10 bits of information to hide in your puzzle, but you must not repeat information that you used in Step 3. DO NOT show where the words are. Fill up empty squares with random letters. Remember to keep a note of where your answers are hidden but do not show your friends. When you have a complete puzzle, exchange it with a friend to solve each other's puzzle.

Step 5

Now make up 10 questions (not "answers" this time) based on the same chapter used in the previous two tasks. Again, you must find NEW information that you have not yet used. Now it's getting hard to find that new information! Again, give your questions to a friend to answer.

Step 6

As you have been doing the puzzles, your brain has been actively searching for new information. Now write a NEW LIST that contains only the new information you have discovered when doing the puzzles. Your new list is the one to look at repeatedly for short bursts over the next few days. Try to remember more and more of it without looking at it. After a few days, you should be able to add words from your second list to your first list as you increase the information in your long-term memory.

FINALLY! Be inspired...

Make a list of different revision ideas and beside each one write **THINGS I HAVE** tried, **THINGS I WILL** try and **THINGS I MIGHT** try. Don't be scared of trying something new.

And remember – "FAIL TO PREPARE AND PREPARE TO FAIL!"

NATIONAL 5

2016

FOR OFFICIAL USE

National
Qualifications
2016

Mark

X747/75/01

Mathematics
Paper 1
(Non-Calculator)

THURSDAY, 12 MAY

1:00 PM – 2:00 PM

Fill in these boxes and read what is printed below.

Full name of centre

Town

Forename(s)

Surname

Number of seat

Date of birth

| Day | Month | Year | Scottish candidate number |

Total marks — 40

Attempt ALL questions.

You may NOT use a calculator.

Full credit will be given only to solutions which contain appropriate working.

State the units for your answer where appropriate.

Write your answers clearly in the spaces provided in this booklet. Additional space for answers is provided at the end of this booklet. If you use this space you must clearly identify the question number you are attempting.

Use **blue** or **black** ink.

Before leaving the examination room you must give this booklet to the Invigilator; if you do not, you may lose all the marks for this paper.

FORMULAE LIST

The roots of $ax^2 + bx + c = 0$ are $x = \dfrac{-b \pm \sqrt{(b^2 - 4ac)}}{2a}$

Sine rule: $\dfrac{a}{\sin A} = \dfrac{b}{\sin B} = \dfrac{c}{\sin C}$

Cosine rule: $a^2 = b^2 + c^2 - 2bc\cos A$ or $\cos A = \dfrac{b^2 + c^2 - a^2}{2bc}$

Area of a triangle: $A = \tfrac{1}{2}ab\sin C$

Volume of a sphere: $V = \tfrac{4}{3}\pi r^3$

Volume of a cone: $V = \tfrac{1}{3}\pi r^2 h$

Volume of a pyramid: $V = \tfrac{1}{3}Ah$

Standard deviation: $s = \sqrt{\dfrac{\Sigma(x - \bar{x})^2}{n - 1}}$

or $s = \sqrt{\dfrac{\Sigma x^2 - \dfrac{(\Sigma x)^2}{n}}{n - 1}}$, where n is the sample size.

MARKS | DO NOT WRITE IN THIS MARGIN

Total marks — 40

Attempt ALL questions

1. Given $\mathbf{p} = \begin{pmatrix} 4 \\ -6 \end{pmatrix}$ and $\mathbf{q} = \begin{pmatrix} -5 \\ -1 \end{pmatrix}$.

   Find the resultant vector $\frac{1}{2}\mathbf{p} + \mathbf{q}$.

   Express your answer in component form.   **2**

2. Evaluate $\frac{3}{4}\left(\frac{1}{3} + \frac{2}{7}\right)$.

   Give your answer in its simplest form.   **2**

[Turn over

MARKS | DO NOT WRITE IN THIS MARGIN

3. The diagram shows a sector of a circle, centre C.

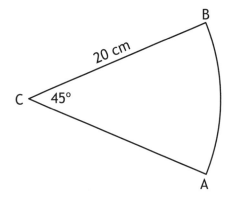

The radius of the circle is 20 centimetres and angle ACB is 45°.

Calculate the area of the sector.

Take π = 3·14.   3

MARKS

4. Charlie is making costumes for a school show.

One day he made 2 cloaks and 3 dresses.

The total amount of material he used was 9·6 square metres.

(a) Write down an equation to illustrate this information.   **1**

(b) The following day Charlie made 3 cloaks and 4 dresses.

The total amount of material he used was 13·3 square metres.

Write down an equation to illustrate this information.   **1**

(c) Calculate the amount of material required to make one cloak and the amount of material required to make one dress.   **4**

[Turn over

MARKS | DO NOT WRITE IN THIS MARGIN

5. A cattle farmer records the weight of some of his calves.

The scattergraph shows the relationship between the age, A months, and the weight, W kilograms, of the calves.

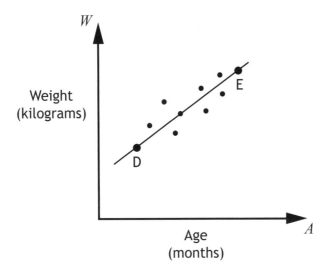

A line of best fit is drawn.

Point D represents a 3 month old calf which weighs 100 kilograms.

Point E represents a 15 month old calf which weighs 340 kilograms.

(a) Find the equation of the line of best fit in terms of A and W.

Give the equation in its simplest form.

3

MARKS | DO NOT WRITE IN THIS MARGIN

5. **(continued)**

(b) Use your equation from part (a) to estimate the weight of a one **year** old calf.

Show your working. 1

6. Determine the nature of the roots of the function $f(x) = 7x^2 + 5x - 1$. 2

[Turn over

MARKS | DO NOT WRITE IN THIS MARGIN

7. The diagram shows a rectangular based pyramid, relative to the coordinate axes.

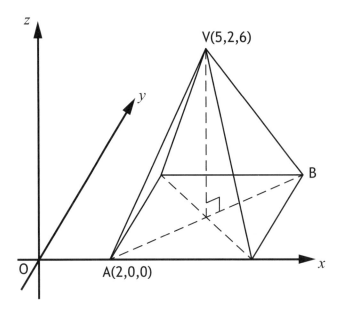

- A is the point (2,0,0).
- V is the point (5,2,6).

(a) Write down the coordinates of B.   1

(b) Calculate the length of edge AV of the pyramid.   3

MARKS DO NOT WRITE IN THIS MARGIN

8. Solve the equation

$$\frac{2x}{3} - \frac{5}{6} = 2x.$$

Give your answer in its simplest form.

3

9. The function $f(x)$ is defined by $f(x) = \dfrac{2}{\sqrt{x}}, \quad x > 0.$

Express $f(5)$ as a fraction with a rational denominator.

2

[Turn over

MARKS | DO NOT WRITE IN THIS MARGIN

10. Sketch the graph of $y = (x-3)^2 + 1$.

On your sketch, show clearly the coordinates of the turning point and the point of intersection with the y-axis.

3

MARKS | DO NOT WRITE IN THIS MARGIN

11. Simplify

$$\tan^2 x^\circ \, \cos^2 x^\circ \, .$$

Show your working.   2

[Turn over

MARKS | DO NOT WRITE IN THIS MARGIN

12. The diagrams below show a rectangle and a triangle.

All measurements are in centimetres.

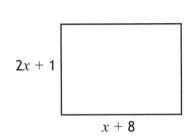

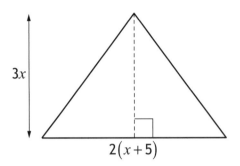

(a) Find an expression for the area of the **rectangle**.

1

(b) Given that the area of the rectangle is equal to the area of the triangle, show that $x^2 - 2x - 8 = 0$.

3

MARKS | DO NOT WRITE IN THIS MARGIN

12. **(continued)**

(c) Hence find, **algebraically**, the length and breadth of the rectangle.

3

[END OF QUESTION PAPER]

MARKS DO NOT WRITE IN THIS MARGIN

ADDITIONAL SPACE FOR ANSWERS

ADDITIONAL SPACE FOR ANSWERS

MARKS | DO NOT WRITE IN THIS MARGIN

ADDITIONAL SPACE FOR ANSWERS

N5

National
Qualifications
2016

Mark

X747/75/02

**Mathematics
Paper 2**

THURSDAY, 12 MAY

2:20 PM — 3:50 PM

Fill in these boxes and read what is printed below.

Full name of centre

Town

Forename(s)

Surname

Number of seat

Date of birth

Day   Month   Year

Scottish candidate number

Total marks — 50

Attempt ALL questions.

You may use a calculator.

Full credit will be given only to solutions which contain appropriate working.

State the units for your answer where appropriate.

Write your answers clearly in the spaces provided in this booklet. Additional space for answers is provided at the end of this booklet. If you use this space you must clearly identify the question number you are attempting.

Use **blue** or **black** ink.

Before leaving the examination room you must give this booklet to the Invigilator; if you do not, you may lose all the marks for this paper.

FORMULAE LIST

The roots of $ax^2 + bx + c = 0$ are $x = \dfrac{-b \pm \sqrt{(b^2 - 4ac)}}{2a}$

Sine rule: $\dfrac{a}{\sin A} = \dfrac{b}{\sin B} = \dfrac{c}{\sin C}$

Cosine rule: $a^2 = b^2 + c^2 - 2bc\cos A$ or $\cos A = \dfrac{b^2 + c^2 - a^2}{2bc}$

Area of a triangle: $A = \frac{1}{2}ab\sin C$

Volume of a sphere: $V = \frac{4}{3}\pi r^3$

Volume of a cone: $V = \frac{1}{3}\pi r^2 h$

Volume of a pyramid: $V = \frac{1}{3}Ah$

Standard deviation: $s = \sqrt{\dfrac{\Sigma(x - \bar{x})^2}{n-1}}$

or $s = \sqrt{\dfrac{\Sigma x^2 - \dfrac{(\Sigma x)^2}{n}}{n-1}}$, where n is the sample size.

MARKS | DO NOT WRITE IN THIS MARGIN

Total marks — 50

Attempt ALL questions

1. A drinks manufacturer is reducing the sugar content of one of their fizzy drinks by 8% per year over the next 3 years.

   The sugar content of a standard can is currently 35 grams.

   Calculate the sugar content of a standard can after 3 years. **3**

2. A pollen sample weighs 12 grams
   and contains $1\cdot5 \times 10^9$ pollen grains.

   Calculate the weight of **one** pollen grain in grams.
   Give your answer in scientific notation. **2**

[Turn over

MARKS | DO NOT WRITE IN THIS MARGIN

3. The diagram below shows parallelogram ABCD.

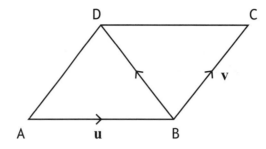

$\overrightarrow{AB}$ represents vector **u** and $\overrightarrow{BC}$ represents vector **v**.

Express $\overrightarrow{BD}$ in terms of **u** and **v**.

1

4. Factorise fully $3x^2 - 48$.

2

MARKS | DO NOT WRITE IN THIS MARGIN

5. The diagram below shows a circle, centre O.

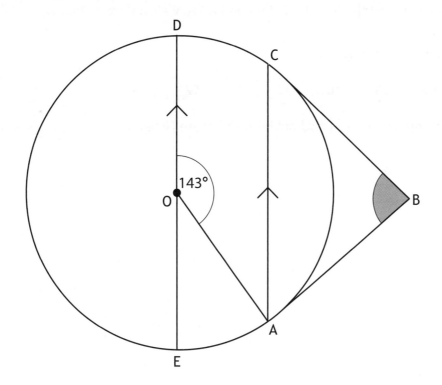

- AB and CB are tangents to the circle.
- AC and ED are parallel.
- Angle AOD is 143°.

Calculate the size of angle ABC.

3

[Turn over

MARKS

6. Jack called his internet provider on six occasions to report connection problems.

On each occasion he noted the length of time he had to wait before speaking to an adviser.

The times (in minutes) were as follows:

13   16   10   22   5   12

(a) Calculate the mean and standard deviation of these times.   4

MARKS | DO NOT WRITE IN THIS MARGIN

6.   (continued)

(b) Sophie also called the same internet provider, on several occasions, to report connection problems.

Her mean waiting time was 15 minutes and the standard deviation was 4·3 minutes.

Make two valid comments comparing Sophie's waiting times with Jack's waiting times.

2

[Turn over

MARKS | DO NOT WRITE IN THIS MARGIN

7. A carton is in the shape of a large cone with a small cone removed.

   The large cone has diameter of 32 cm and height 24 cm.

   The small cone has diameter of 18 cm and height 13·5 cm.

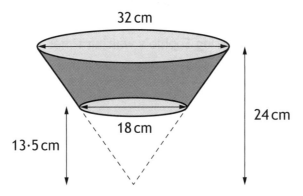

Calculate the volume of the carton.

Give your answer correct to 2 significant figures.   5

MARKS | DO NOT WRITE IN THIS MARGIN

8. A set of stepladders has legs 150 centimetres and 140 centimetres long.

When the stepladder is fully open, the angle between the longer leg and the ground is 66°.

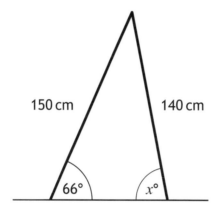

150 cm   140 cm

66° $x°$

Calculate $x°$, the size of the angle between the shorter leg and the ground.   3

[Turn over

MARKS | DO NOT WRITE IN THIS MARGIN

9. Express $x^2 + 8x - 7$ in the form $(x + a)^2 + b$.

2

10. Simplify $\left(n^2\right)^3 \times n^{-10}$.

Give your answer with a **positive** power.

3

MARKS | DO NOT WRITE IN THIS MARGIN

11. Two pictures are mathematically similar in shape.

100 cm

60 cm

The cost of each picture is proportional to its area.

The large picture costs £13·75.

Find the cost of the small picture.

3

[Turn over

12. Change the subject of the formula $L = \sqrt{4kt - p}$ to k.

3

13. Express

$$\frac{3}{x-2} + \frac{5}{x+1}, \qquad x \neq 2, \, x \neq -1$$

as a single fraction in its simplest form.

3

MARKS | DO NOT WRITE IN THIS MARGIN

14. Solve the equation $2 \tan x° + 5 = -4$, for $0 \le x \le 360$.

3

[Turn over

MARKS | DO NOT WRITE IN THIS MARGIN

15. This perfume bottle has a label in the shape of part of a circle.

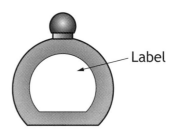

Label

A diagram of the label is shown below.

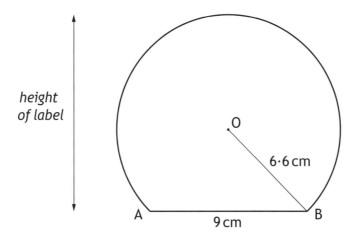

height of label

O

6·6 cm

A

9 cm

B

- The centre of the circle is O.
- The chord AB is 9 centimetres.
- The radius OB is 6·6 centimetres.

Find the height of the label.

4

MARKS | DO NOT WRITE IN THIS MARGIN

16. In the diagram below:

- DE is perpendicular to AC.
- AD = 4 centimetres.
- DB = 6 centimetres.
- AE = EC = 3 centimetres.

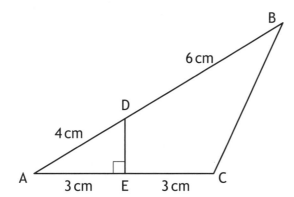

Calculate the length of BC.

Give your answer correct to one decimal place.   **4**

[END OF QUESTION PAPER]

ADDITIONAL SPACE FOR ANSWERS

Page sixteen

MARKS

DO NOT
WRITE IN
THIS
MARGIN

ADDITIONAL SPACE FOR ANSWERS

MARKS | DO NOT WRITE IN THIS MARGIN

ADDITIONAL SPACE FOR ANSWERS

NATIONAL 5

2017

FOR OFFICIAL USE

N5

National Qualifications 2017

Mark

X747/75/01

Mathematics Paper 1 (Non-Calculator)

FRIDAY, 5 MAY

1:00 PM — 2:00 PM

Fill in these boxes and read what is printed below.

Full name of centre

Town

Forename(s)

Surname

Number of seat

Date of birth

Day   Month   Year   Scottish candidate number

Total marks — 40

Attempt ALL questions.

You may NOT use a calculator.

Full credit will be given only to solutions which contain appropriate working.

State the units for your answer where appropriate.

Write your answers clearly in the spaces provided in this booklet. Additional space for answers is provided at the end of this booklet. If you use this space you must clearly identify the question number you are attempting.

Use **blue** or **black** ink.

Before leaving the examination room you must give this book to the Invigilator; if you do not, you may lose all the marks for this paper.

FORMULAE LIST

The roots of $ax^2 + bx + c = 0$ are $x = \dfrac{-b \pm \sqrt{(b^2 - 4ac)}}{2a}$

Sine rule: $\dfrac{a}{\sin A} = \dfrac{b}{\sin B} = \dfrac{c}{\sin C}$

Cosine rule: $a^2 = b^2 + c^2 - 2bc\cos A$ or $\cos A = \dfrac{b^2 + c^2 - a^2}{2bc}$

Area of a triangle: $A = \frac{1}{2}ab\sin C$

Volume of a sphere: $V = \frac{4}{3}\pi r^3$

Volume of a cone: $V = \frac{1}{3}\pi r^2 h$

Volume of a pyramid: $V = \frac{1}{3}Ah$

Standard deviation: $s = \sqrt{\dfrac{\Sigma(x - \bar{x})^2}{n-1}}$

or $s = \sqrt{\dfrac{\Sigma x^2 - \dfrac{(\Sigma x)^2}{n}}{n-1}}$, where n is the sample size.

MARKS | DO NOT WRITE IN THIS MARGIN

Total marks — 40

Attempt ALL questions

1. Given that $f(x) = x^2 + 3x$, evaluate $f(-5)$. **2**

2. The number of calls received by the police was recorded over 10 days. The results are shown below.

   198   216   218   230   232   247   248   250   265   267

   Find the semi-interquartile range of this data. **2**

[Turn over

3. Evaluate $1\frac{5}{6} \div \frac{3}{4}$.

   Give your answer in its simplest form.

   2

4. Expand and simplify $(2x+3)(x^2 - 4x + 1)$.

   3

MARKS | DO NOT WRITE IN THIS MARGIN

5. The diagram shows a square-based pyramid placed on top of a cube, relative to the coordinate axes.

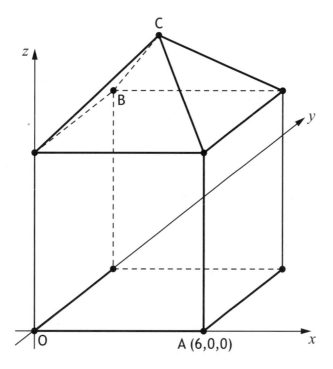

The height of the pyramid is half of the height of the cube.

A is the point (6,0,0).

The point C is directly above the centre of the base.

Write down the coordinates of B and C.   2

[Turn over

MARKS | DO NOT WRITE IN THIS MARGIN

6. The diagram below shows the straight line joining points A and B.

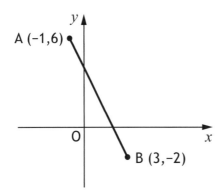

Find the equation of the line AB.

Give the equation in its simplest form.

3

MARKS | DO NOT WRITE IN THIS MARGIN

7. In triangle DEF:

- DE = 8 centimetres

- EF = 12 centimetres

- $\sin E = \dfrac{2}{3}$

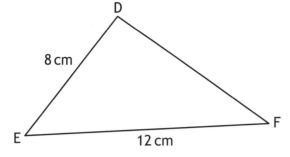

Calculate the area of triangle DEF.   2

[Turn over

MARKS | DO NOT WRITE IN THIS MARGIN

8. Solve, algebraically, the inequality

$$19 + x > 15 + 3(x - 2).$$

3

MARKS | DO NOT WRITE IN THIS MARGIN

9. In the diagram shown below:

    • ABE is a tangent to the circle centre O

    • Angle DBE is 58°

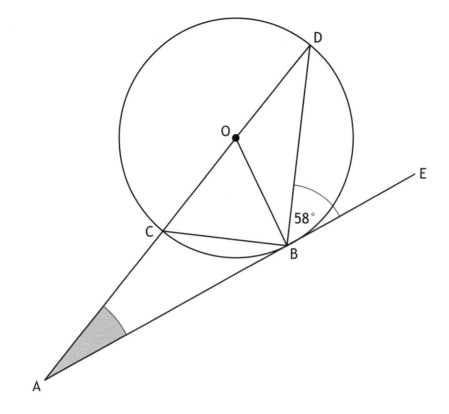

Calculate the size of angle CAB.   3

[Turn over

MARKS | DO NOT WRITE IN THIS MARGIN

10. Change the subject of the formula $F = \dfrac{t^2 + 4b}{c}$ to b.

3

11. Express $\dfrac{3}{a^2} - \dfrac{2}{a}$, $a \neq 0$, as a single fraction in its simplest form.

2

MARKS | DO NOT WRITE IN THIS MARGIN

12. Gym members are asked to fill out a questionnaire to rate the quality of service provided.

They are asked to give a rating on a scale of 1 to 6.

The ratings given by five members were as follows:

$$1 \quad 4 \quad 6 \quad 3 \quad 6$$

In its simplest form, the standard deviation of these ratings can be written as $\dfrac{a\sqrt{b}}{2}$.

Find the values of a and b. 4

[Turn over

MARKS | DO NOT WRITE IN THIS MARGIN

13. The graph below shows two straight lines with the equations:

- $3x - y = 2$

- $x + 3y = 19$

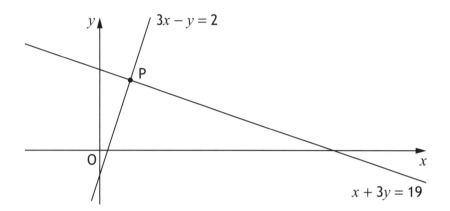

The lines intersect at the point P.

Find, **algebraically**, the coordinates of P.   3

MARKS | DO NOT WRITE IN THIS MARGIN

14. The graph below shows a parabola with equation of the form $y = (x+a)^2 + b$.

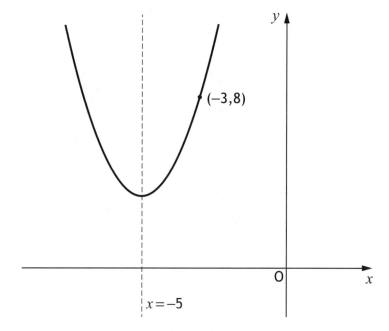

The equation of the axis of symmetry of the parabola is $x = -5$.

(a) State the value of a.   1

The point $(-3,8)$ lies on the parabola.

(b) Calculate the value of b.   2

[Turn over for next question

MARKS | DO NOT WRITE IN THIS MARGIN

15. In the diagram below:

- TS is parallel to QR
- TS = 5 centimetres
- QR = 7 centimetres
- SR = 2·6 centimetres

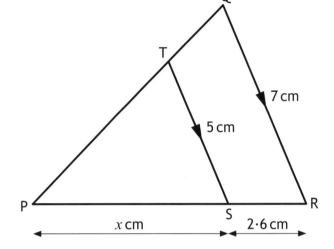

The length of PS is x centimetres.

Calculate the value of x.   3

[END OF QUESTION PAPER]

MARKS DO NOT WRITE IN THIS MARGIN

ADDITIONAL SPACE FOR ANSWERS

ADDITIONAL SPACE FOR ANSWERS

FOR OFFICIAL USE

N5

National Qualifications 2017

Mark

X747/75/02

Mathematics Paper 2

FRIDAY, 5 MAY

2:20 PM — 3:50 PM

Fill in these boxes and read what is printed below.

Full name of centre

Town

Forename(s)

Surname

Number of seat

Date of birth

Day   Month   Year

Scottish candidate number

Total marks — 50

Attempt ALL questions.

You may use a calculator.

Full credit will be given only to solutions which contain appropriate working.

State the units for your answer where appropriate.

Write your answers clearly in the spaces provided in this booklet. Additional space for answers is provided at the end of this booklet. If you use this space you must clearly identify the question number you are attempting.

Use **blue** or **black** ink.

Before leaving the examination room you must give this book to the Invigilator; if you do not, you may lose all the marks for this paper.

FORMULAE LIST

The roots of $ax^2 + bx + c = 0$ are $x = \dfrac{-b \pm \sqrt{(b^2 - 4ac)}}{2a}$

Sine rule: $\dfrac{a}{\sin A} = \dfrac{b}{\sin B} = \dfrac{c}{\sin C}$

Cosine rule: $a^2 = b^2 + c^2 - 2bc \cos A$ or $\cos A = \dfrac{b^2 + c^2 - a^2}{2bc}$

Area of a triangle: $A = \frac{1}{2}ab \sin C$

Volume of a sphere: $V = \frac{4}{3}\pi r^3$

Volume of a cone: $V = \frac{1}{3}\pi r^2 h$

Volume of a pyramid: $V = \frac{1}{3}Ah$

Standard deviation: $s = \sqrt{\dfrac{\Sigma(x - \bar{x})^2}{n - 1}}$

or $s = \sqrt{\dfrac{\Sigma x^2 - \dfrac{(\Sigma x)^2}{n}}{n - 1}}$, where n is the sample size.

MARKS

Total marks — 50

Attempt ALL questions

1. Find $|\mathbf{v}|$, the magnitude of vector $\mathbf{v} = \begin{pmatrix} 18 \\ -14 \\ 3 \end{pmatrix}$.   2

2. A necklace is valued at £1200.

   Its value is expected to increase by 4·5% per year over the next 3 years.

   Calculate the expected value of the necklace after this time.

   Give your answer to the nearest pound.   3

[Turn over

MARKS | DO NOT WRITE IN THIS MARGIN

3. A piece of land is in the shape of a triangle as shown.

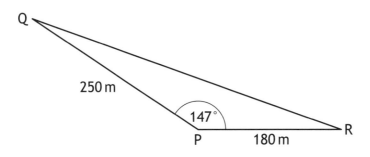

- PQ = 250 metres
- PR = 180 metres
- angle QPR = 147°

The owner wishes to build a fence along the side QR.

Calculate the length of the fence.　　　　3

MARKS | DO NOT WRITE IN THIS MARGIN

4. Solve the equation $2x^2 + 5x - 4 = 0$.

   Give your answers correct to one decimal place.   **3**

5. A theatre group sold 4830 tickets for their show.

   This was 15% more than they sold last year.

   How many tickets did they sell last year?   **3**

[Turn over

6. A spherical sweet is made by coating a caramel sphere evenly with chocolate.

   A cross-section of the sweet is shown below.

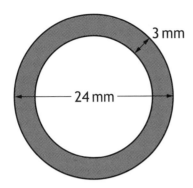

   The diameter of the sweet is 24 millimetres and the thickness of the chocolate coating is 3 millimetres.

   Calculate the volume of the chocolate coating.   5

   Give your answer correct to 3 significant figures.

MARKS | DO NOT WRITE IN THIS MARGIN

7. Triangles A and B are shown below.

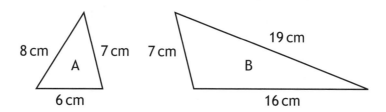

The triangles are placed together to form the larger triangle shown below.

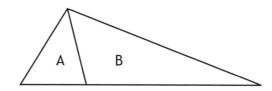

Is this larger triangle right-angled?

Justify your answer.

3

[Turn over

MARKS | DO NOT WRITE IN THIS MARGIN

8. In the diagram below, $\overrightarrow{RQ}$ and $\overrightarrow{PQ}$ represent the vectors **c** and **d** respectively.

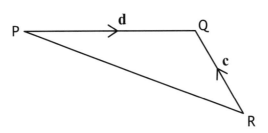

(a) Express $\overrightarrow{PR}$ in terms of **c** and **d**.

1

The line QP is extended to T.

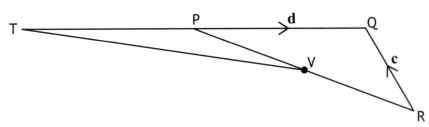

- TP = PQ
- V is the midpoint of PR

(b) Express $\overrightarrow{TV}$ in terms of **c** and **d**.

Give your answer in simplest form.

2

MARKS | DO NOT WRITE IN THIS MARGIN

9. (a) Factorise $4x^2 - 25$.

1

(b) Hence simplify $\dfrac{4x^2 - 25}{2x^2 - x - 10}$.

3

[Turn over

1

MARKS | DO NOT WRITE IN THIS MARGIN

10. In the diagram below D, E and F represent the positions of Dunbridge, Earlsford and Fairtown respectively.

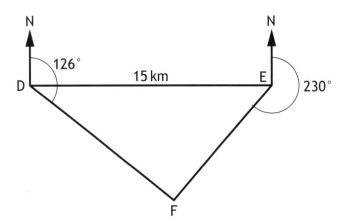

Dunbridge is 15 kilometres west of Earlsford.

From Dunbridge, the bearing of Fairtown is 126°.

From Earlsford the bearing of Fairtown is 230°.

Calculate the distance between Dunbridge and Fairtown.   4

Do not use a scale drawing.

MARKS | DO NOT WRITE IN THIS MARGIN

11. A straight line has equation $3x - 5y - 10 = 0$.

Find the gradient of this line.

2

12. Express $\dfrac{1}{\sqrt[3]{x}}$ in the form x^n.

2

[Turn over

MARKS | DO NOT WRITE IN THIS MARGIN

13. Two identical shapes are used to form a logo.

Each shape is part of a circle.

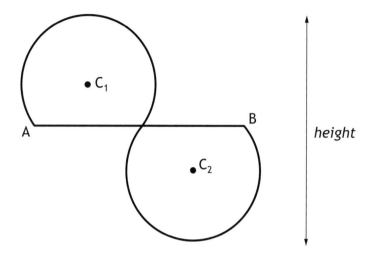

- The circles have centres C_1 and C_2.
- The radius of each circle is 14 centimetres.
- The logo has half-turn symmetry about the mid-point of AB.
- AB is 48 centimetres long.

Calculate the height of the logo.

4

MARKS | DO NOT WRITE IN THIS MARGIN

14. The diagram below shows part of a circle, centre O.

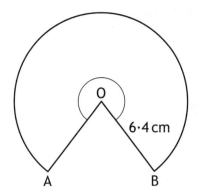

The radius of the circle is 6·4 centimetres.

Major arc AB has length 31·5 centimetres.

Calculate the size of the reflex angle AOB.   3

[Turn over

MARKS | DO NOT WRITE IN THIS MARGIN

15. A wind turbine has three blades as shown below.

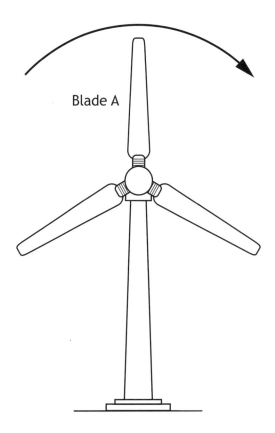

Blade A

The height, h metres, of the tip of blade A above the ground in each rotation is given by

$$h = 40 + 23\cos x°, \qquad 0 \leq x < 360$$

where x is the angle blade A has turned clockwise from its vertical position.

(a) Calculate the height of the tip of blade A after it has turned through an angle of 60°.

1

MARKS

DO NOT WRITE IN THIS MARGIN

15.   (continued)

(b)   Find the minimum height of the tip of blade A above the ground.   **1**

(c)   Calculate the values of x for which the tip of blade A is 61 metres above the ground.   **4**

[END OF QUESTION PAPER]

MARKS

ADDITIONAL SPACE FOR ANSWERS

MARKS

ADDITIONAL SPACE FOR ANSWERS

MARKS

ADDITIONAL SPACE FOR ANSWERS

NATIONAL 5

2017 Specimen Question Paper

N5

National
Qualifications
SPECIMEN ONLY

Mark

S847/75/01

Mathematics
Paper 1
(Non-Calculator)

Date — Not applicable

Duration — 1 hour 15 minutes

Fill in these boxes and read what is printed below.

Full name of centre

Town

Forename(s)

Surname

Number of seat

Date of birth

Day	Month	Year	Scottish candidate number

Total marks — 50

Attempt ALL questions.

You may NOT use a calculator.

To earn full marks you must show your working in your answers.

State the units for your answer where appropriate.

Write your answers clearly in the spaces provided in this booklet. Additional space for answers is provided at the end of this booklet. If you use this space you must clearly identify the question number you are attempting.

Use **blue** or **black** ink.

Before leaving the examination room you must give this booklet to the Invigilator; if you do not, you may lose all the marks for this paper.

FORMULAE LIST

The roots of $ax^2 + bx + c = 0$ are $x = \dfrac{-b \pm \sqrt{(b^2 - 4ac)}}{2a}$

Sine rule: $\dfrac{a}{\sin A} = \dfrac{b}{\sin B} = \dfrac{c}{\sin C}$

Cosine rule: $a^2 = b^2 + c^2 - 2bc \cos A$ or $\cos A = \dfrac{b^2 + c^2 - a^2}{2bc}$

Area of a triangle: $A = \frac{1}{2}ab \sin C$

Volume of a sphere: $V = \frac{4}{3}\pi r^3$

Volume of a cone: $V = \frac{1}{3}\pi r^2 h$

Volume of a pyramid: $V = \frac{1}{3}Ah$

Standard deviation: $s = \sqrt{\dfrac{\Sigma(x - \bar{x})^2}{n - 1}}$

or $s = \sqrt{\dfrac{\Sigma x^2 - \dfrac{(\Sigma x)^2}{n}}{n - 1}}$, where n is the sample size.

MARKS | DO NOT WRITE IN THIS MARGIN

Total marks — 50

Attempt ALL questions

1. Evaluate

   $$2\frac{3}{8} \div \frac{5}{16}.$$

   2

2. Solve algebraically the inequality

   $$11 - 2(1 + 3x) < 39.$$

   3

[Turn over

3. Two forces acting on a rocket are represented by vectors **u** and **v**.

$$\mathbf{u} = \begin{pmatrix} 2 \\ -5 \\ -3 \end{pmatrix} \text{ and } \mathbf{v} = \begin{pmatrix} 7 \\ 4 \\ -1 \end{pmatrix}.$$

Calculate $|\mathbf{u} + \mathbf{v}|$, the magnitude of the resultant force.

Express your answer as a surd in its simplest form.   3

MARKS   DO NOT WRITE IN THIS MARGIN

4. The diagram below shows part of the graph of $y = ax^2$.

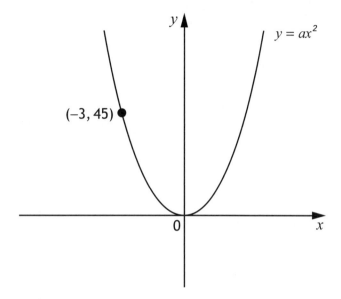

Find the value of a.   **2**

[Turn over

5. Determine the nature of the roots of the function $f(x) = 7x^2 + 5x - 1$.

2

MARKS | DO NOT WRITE IN THIS MARGIN

6. A cattle farmer records the weight of some of his calves.

    The scattergraph shows the relationship between the age, A months, and the weight, W kilograms, of the calves.

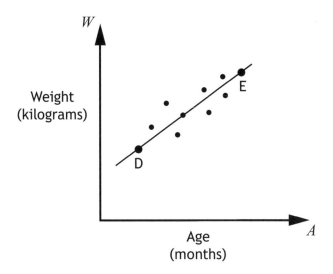

    A line of best fit is drawn.

    Point D represents a 3-month-old calf which weighs 100 kilograms.

    Point E represents a 15-month-old calf which weighs 340 kilograms.

    (a) Find the equation of the line of best fit in terms of A and W.

         Give the equation in its simplest form.   **3**

[**Turn over**

MARKS   DO NOT WRITE IN THIS MARGIN

6. (continued)

(b) Use your equation from part (a) to estimate the weight of a 1-**year**-old calf.

Show your working.   **1**

MARKS

7. Ten couples took part in a dance competition.

The couples were given a score in each round.

The scores in the first round were

16   27   12   18   26   21   27   22   18   17

(a) Calculate the median and semi-interquartile range of these scores.   **3**

(b) In the second round, the median was 26 and the semi-interquartile range was 2·5.

Make two valid comparisons between the scores in the first and second rounds.   **2**

[Turn over

MARKS | DO NOT WRITE IN THIS MARGIN

8. Two groups of people go to a theatre.

   Bill buys tickets for 5 adults and 3 children.

   The total cost of his tickets is £158·25.

   (a) Write down an equation to illustrate this information.   **1**

   (b) Ben buys tickets for 3 adults and 2 children.

   The total cost of his tickets is £98.

   Write down an equation to illustrate this information.   **1**

   (c) Calculate the cost of a ticket for an adult and the cost of a ticket for a child.   **4**

MARKS

9. 480 000 tickets were sold for a tennis tournament last year.

This represents 80% of all the available tickets.

Calculate the total number of tickets that were available for this tournament.   **3**

10. The function $f(x)$ is defined by $f(x) = \dfrac{2}{\sqrt{x}}, \quad x > 0.$

Express $f(5)$ as a fraction with a rational denominator.   **2**

[Turn over

MARKS | DO NOT WRITE IN THIS MARGIN

11. In the diagram, OABCDE is a regular hexagon with centre M.

Vectors **a** and **b** are represented by $\overrightarrow{OA}$ and $\overrightarrow{OB}$ respectively.

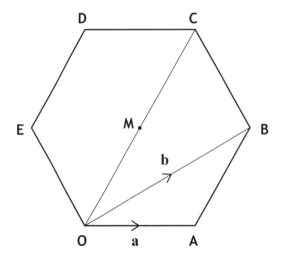

(a) Express $\overrightarrow{AB}$ in terms of **a** and **b**.   1

(b) Express $\overrightarrow{OC}$ in terms of **a** and **b**.   1

MARKS

12. Part of the graph of $y = a \sin bx°$ is shown in the diagram.

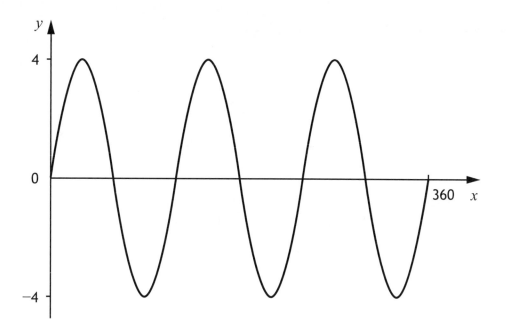

State the values of a and b.

2

[**Turn over**

MARKS

DO NOT WRITE IN THIS MARGIN

13. A parabola has equation $y = x^2 - 8x + 19$.

(a) Write the equation in the form $y = (x - p)^2 + q$.

2

(b) Sketch the graph of $y = x^2 - 8x + 19$, showing the coordinates of the turning point and the point of intersection with the y-axis.

3

MARKS | DO NOT WRITE IN THIS MARGIN

14. Express

$$\frac{4}{x+2} - \frac{3}{x-4}, \qquad x \neq -2,\ x \neq 4$$

as a single fraction in its simplest form.

3

15. Simplify

$$\tan^2 x^\circ \cos^2 x^\circ.$$

Show your working.

2

[Turn over

MARKS | DO NOT WRITE IN THIS MARGIN

16. A cylindrical pipe has water in it as shown.

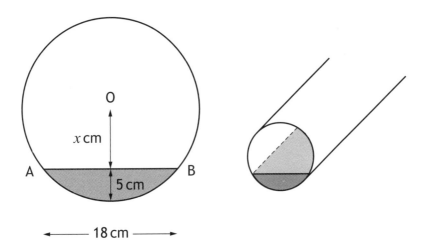

The depth of the water at the deepest point is 5 centimetres.

The width of the water surface, AB, is 18 centimetres.

The radius of the pipe is r centimetres.

The distance from the centre, O, of the pipe to the water surface is x centimetres.

(a) Write down an expression for x in terms of r.   1

(b) Calculate r, the radius of the pipe.   3

[END OF SPECIMEN QUESTION PAPER]

ADDITIONAL SPACE FOR ANSWERS

MARKS

DO NOT WRITE IN THIS MARGIN

ADDITIONAL SPACE FOR ANSWERS

FOR OFFICIAL USE

N5

National Qualifications
SPECIMEN ONLY

Mark

S847/75/02

Mathematics
Paper 2

Date — Not applicable

Duration — 1 hour 50 minutes

Fill in these boxes and read what is printed below.

Full name of centre

Town

Forename(s)

Surname

Number of seat

Date of birth

Day	Month	Year	Scottish candidate number

Total marks — 60

Attempt ALL questions.

You may use a calculator.

To earn full marks you must show your working in your answers.

State the units for your answer where appropriate.

Write your answers clearly in the spaces provided in this booklet. Additional space for answers is provided at the end of this booklet. If you use this space you must clearly identify the question number you are attempting.

Use **blue** or **black** ink.

Before leaving the examination room you must give this booklet to the Invigilator; if you do not, you may lose all the marks for this paper.

FORMULAE LIST

The roots of $ax^2 + bx + c = 0$ are $x = \dfrac{-b \pm \sqrt{(b^2 - 4ac)}}{2a}$

Sine rule: $\dfrac{a}{\sin A} = \dfrac{b}{\sin B} = \dfrac{c}{\sin C}$

Cosine rule: $a^2 = b^2 + c^2 - 2bc \cos A$ or $\cos A = \dfrac{b^2 + c^2 - a^2}{2bc}$

Area of a triangle: $A = \frac{1}{2} ab \sin C$

Volume of a sphere: $V = \frac{4}{3} \pi r^3$

Volume of a cone: $V = \frac{1}{3} \pi r^2 h$

Volume of a pyramid: $V = \frac{1}{3} Ah$

Standard deviation: $s = \sqrt{\dfrac{\Sigma(x - \bar{x})^2}{n-1}}$

or $s = \sqrt{\dfrac{\Sigma x^2 - \dfrac{(\Sigma x)^2}{n}}{n-1}}$, where n is the sample size.

MARKS | DO NOT WRITE IN THIS MARGIN

Total marks — 60

Attempt ALL questions

1. Beth normally cycles a total distance of 64 miles per week.

   She increases her total distance by 15% each week for the next three weeks.

   How many miles does she cycle in the third week?   **3**

   Give your answer to the nearest mile.

2. There are 3×10^5 platelets per millilitre of blood.

   On average, a person has 5·5 litres of blood.

   On average, how many platelets does a person have in their blood?

   Give your answer in scientific notation.   **2**

[Turn over

MARKS | DO NOT WRITE IN THIS MARGIN

3. Expand and simplify

$(2x+3)(x^2-4x+1)$.

3

4. The diagram shows a cube placed on top of a cuboid, relative to the coordinate axes.

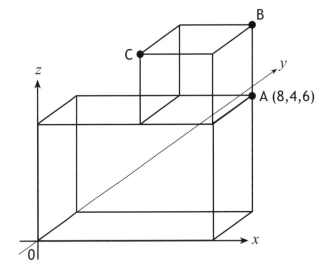

A is the point (8,4,6).

Write down the coordinates of B and C.

2

MARKS | DO NOT WRITE IN THIS MARGIN

5. In triangle PQR, PQ = 8 centimetres, QR = 3 centimetres and angle PQR = 120°.

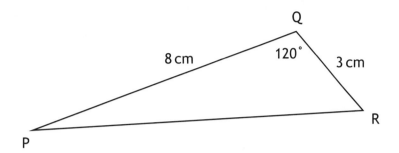

Calculate the length of PR.   **3**

[Turn over

MARKS | DO NOT WRITE IN THIS MARGIN

6. A child's toy is in the shape of a hemisphere with a cone on top, as shown in the diagram.

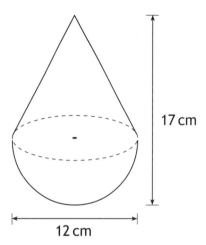

17 cm

12 cm

The toy is 12 centimetres wide and 17 centimetres high.

Calculate the volume of the toy.

Give your answer correct to 2 significant figures.

5

MARKS | DO NOT WRITE IN THIS MARGIN

7. Screenwash is available in bottles which are mathematically similar.

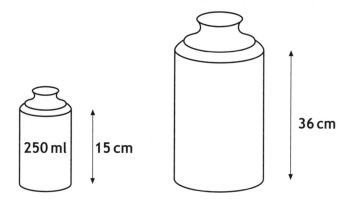

The smaller bottle has a height of 15 centimetres and a volume of 250 millilitres.

The larger bottle has a height of 36 centimetres.

Calculate the volume of the larger bottle.   3

[Turn over

MARKS | DO NOT WRITE IN THIS MARGIN

8. Simplify $\dfrac{n^5 \times 10n}{2n^2}$.

3

MARKS | DO NOT WRITE IN THIS MARGIN

9. (a) A straight line has equation $4x + 3y = 12$.

Find the gradient of this line. **2**

(b) State the coordinates of the point where the line crosses the y-axis. **1**

[Turn over

10. The top of a table is in the shape of a regular hexagon.

The three diagonals of the hexagon, which are shown as dotted lines in the diagram below, each have length 40 centimetres.

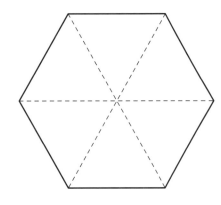

Calculate the area of the top of the table.   4

11. A cone is formed from a paper circle with a sector removed as shown.

The radius of the paper circle is 30 centimetres.

Angle AOB is 110°.

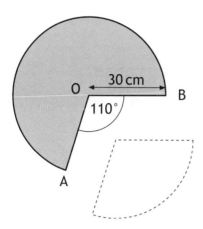 

(a) Calculate the area of the sector removed from the circle.

3

(b) Calculate the circumference of the base of the cone.

3

[Turn over

12. Part of the graph $y = 3\cos x° - 1$ is shown below.

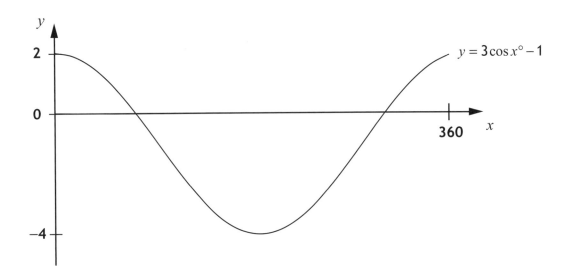

Calculate the x-coordinates of the points where the graph cuts the x-axis.　4

13. Simplify $\dfrac{x^2 - 4x}{x^2 + x - 20}$.

3

[Turn over

14. Change the subject of the formula $s = ut + \dfrac{1}{2}at^2$ to a.

3

MARKS | DO NOT WRITE IN THIS MARGIN

15. A yacht sails from a harbour H to a point C, then to a point D as shown below.

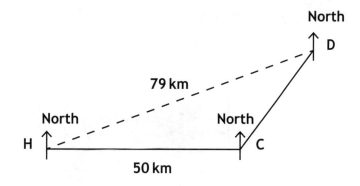

C is 50 kilometres due east of H.

D is on a bearing of 040° from C and is 79 kilometres from H.

(a) Calculate the size of angle CDH.   4

(b) Hence, calculate the bearing on which the yacht must sail to return directly to the harbour.   2

[Turn over

MARKS | DO NOT WRITE IN THIS MARGIN

16. A rectangular picture measuring 9 centimetres by 13 centimetres is placed on a rectangular piece of card.

The area of the card is 270 square centimetres.

There is a border x centimetres wide on all sides of the picture.

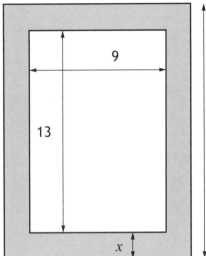

(a) (i) Write down an expression for the length of the card in terms of x. **1**

(ii) Hence show that $4x^2 + 44x - 153 = 0$. **2**

MARKS DO NOT WRITE IN THIS MARGIN

16. (continued)

(b) Calculate x, the width of the border.

Give your answer correct to one decimal place.

4

[END OF SPECIMEN QUESTION PAPER]

MARKS

DO NOT
WRITE IN
THIS
MARGIN

ADDITIONAL SPACE FOR ANSWERS

MARKS

ADDITIONAL SPACE FOR ANSWERS

MARKS | DO NOT WRITE IN THIS MARGIN

ADDITIONAL SPACE FOR ANSWERS

Page twenty

NATIONAL 5

Answers

NATIONAL 5 MATHEMATICS 2016

Paper 1

1. $\begin{bmatrix} -3 \\ -4 \end{bmatrix}$

2. $\dfrac{13}{28}$

3. 157 cm²

4. (a) $2c + 3d = 9 \cdot 6$

   (b) $3c + 4d = 13 \cdot 3$

   (c) A cloak requires 1·5 m² of material; a dress requires 2·2 m² of material

5. (a) $W = 20A + 40$

   (b) $20 \times 12 + 40 = 280$ kg

6. Real and distinct

7. (a) (8, 4, 0)

   (b) 7

8. $x = -\dfrac{5}{8}$

9. $\dfrac{2\sqrt{5}}{5}$

10.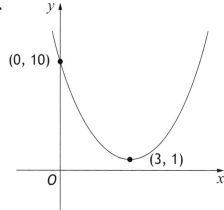

11. $\sin^2 x°$

12. (a) $(2x + 1)(x + 8)$

    (b) $2x^2 + 16x + x + 8 = 3x^2 + 15x$

    $\Rightarrow x^2 - 2x - 8 = 0$

    (c) 12 cm and 9 cm

Paper 2

1. 27(·25408) grams

2. 8×10^{-9} grams

3. $\mathbf{v} - \mathbf{u}$

4. $3(x + 4)(x - 4)$

5. ABC = 74°

6. (a) Mean = 13 minutes, standard deviation = 5·7 minutes

   (b) Valid statements, eg, on average Sophie's waiting time was longer; Sophie's waiting times were more consistent

7. 5300 cm³

8. 78°

9. $(x + 4)^2 - 23$

10. $\dfrac{1}{n^4}$

11. £4·95

12. $k = \dfrac{L^2 + p}{4t}$

13. $\dfrac{8x - 7}{(x - 2)(x + 1)}$

14. $x = 102 \cdot 5°,\ 282 \cdot 5°$

15. 11·4 … cm

16. 6·8 cm

NATIONAL 5 MATHEMATICS 2017

Paper 1

1. 10

2. 16

3. $\dfrac{22}{9}$

4. $2x^3 - 5x^2 - 10x + 3$

5. B(0,6,6), C(3,3,9)

6. $y = -2x + 4$

7. 32 cm²

8. $x < 5$

9. 26°

10. $b = \dfrac{Fc - t^2}{4}$ or equivalent

11. $\dfrac{3 - 2a}{a^2}$

12. $a = 3, b = 2$

13. (2·5, 5·5)

14. (a) $a = 5$
    (b) $b = 4$

15. 6·5

Paper 2

1. 23

2. £1369

3. 413 m

4. $x = -3\cdot1, x = 0\cdot6$

5. 4200

6. 4180 mm³

7.

Method 1

$8^2 + 19^2$ and 22^2

$8^2 + 19^2 = 425, 22^2 = 484$

$8^2 + 19^2 \neq 22^2$; No

Method 2

$\cos x° = \dfrac{8^2 + 19^2 - 22^2}{2 \times 8 \times 19}$

$\cos x° = -0\cdot194$

$x = 101\cdot2°$; No

Method 3

$\cos x° = \dfrac{8^2 + 7^2 - 6^2}{2 \times 8 \times 7}$

and $\cos y° = \dfrac{7^2 + 19^2 - 16^2}{2 \times 7 \times 19}$

$\cos x° = 0\cdot6875$ and $\cos y° = 0\cdot5789$

$x° + y° = 46\cdot6° + 54\cdot6° = 101\cdot2°$; No

8. (a) $\mathbf{d} - \mathbf{c}$

   (b) $\dfrac{3}{2}\mathbf{d} - \dfrac{1}{2}\mathbf{c}$

9. (a) $(2x - 5)(2x + 5)$

   (b) $\dfrac{2x + 5}{x + 2}$

10. 9·9 kilometres

11. $\dfrac{3}{5}$ or 0·6

12. $x^{-\frac{1}{3}}$

13. 42·2 centimetres

14. 282°

15. (a) 51·5 metres

    (b) 17 metres

    (c) 24·1° and 335·9°

NATIONAL 5 MATHEMATICS
2017 SPECIMEN QUESTION PAPER

Paper 1

1. $7\frac{3}{5}$

2. $x > -5$

3. $7\sqrt{2}$

4. $a = 5$

5. Two real and distinct roots

6. (a) $W = 20A + 40$

   (b) $20 \times 12 + 40 = 280\,\text{kg}$

7. (a) Median = 19·5, SIQR = 4·5

   (b) Valid comments, eg, on average the second round's scores are higher; the second round's scores are more consistent

8. (a) $5a + 3c = 158\cdot25$

   (b) $3a + 2c = 98$

   (c) Adult ticket costs £22·50
       Child ticket costs £15·25

9. 600000

10. $\dfrac{2\sqrt{5}}{5}$

11. (a) $b - a$ or $-a + b$

    (b) $2(b - a)$ or $2(-a + b)$

12. $a = 4, b = 3$

13. (a) $(x - 4)^2 + 3$

    (b)
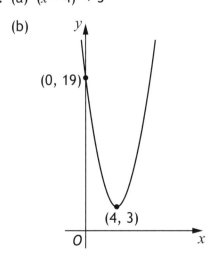

14. $\dfrac{x - 22}{(x + 2)(x - 4)}$

15. $\dfrac{\sin^2 x^\circ}{\cos^2 x^\circ} = \sin^2 x^\circ$

16. (a) $r - 5$

    (b) 10·6

Paper 2

1. 97 miles

2. $1\cdot65 \times 10^9$

3. $2x^3 - 5x^2 - 10x + 3$

4. B(8, 4, 10), C(4, 0, 10)

5. 9·8 cm

6. 870 cm^3

7. 3456 millilitres

8. $5n^4$

9. (a) gradient $= -\dfrac{4}{3}$

   (b) (0,4)

10. 1039·2 cm^2

11. (a) 864 cm^2

    (b) 131 cm

12. 70·5, 289·5

13. $\dfrac{x}{x+5}$

14. $a = \dfrac{2(s - ut)}{t^2}$

15. (a) 29°

    (b) 249°

16. (a) (i) $2x + 13$

       (ii) $4x^2 + 44x + 117 = 270$

           $\Rightarrow 4x^2 + 44x - 153 = 0$

    (b) 2·8 cm

Acknowledgements

Permission has been sought from all relevant copyright holders and Hodder Gibson is grateful for the use of the following:

Image © g215/Shutterstock.com (2016 Paper 2 page 3);
Image © Le Do/Shutterstock.com (2016 Paper 2 page 9);
Image © han871111/Shutterstock.com (2016 Paper 2 page 11).